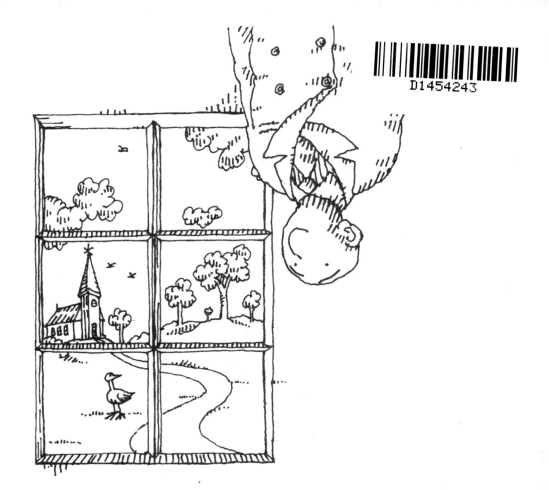

ODD VISIONS AND BIZARRE SIGHTS

SIMON BOND

methuen

First published in 1983
Reprinted 1983
by Methuen London Ltd
11 New Fetter Lane, London EC4P 4EE
Copyright © Polycarp Ltd 1983

ISBN 0 413 52870 7

Printed in Great Britain by
Richard Clay (The Chaucer Press) Ltd, Bungay, Suffolk

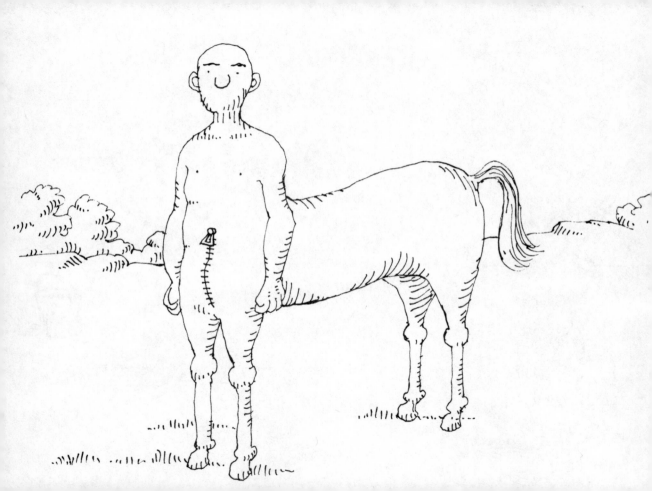

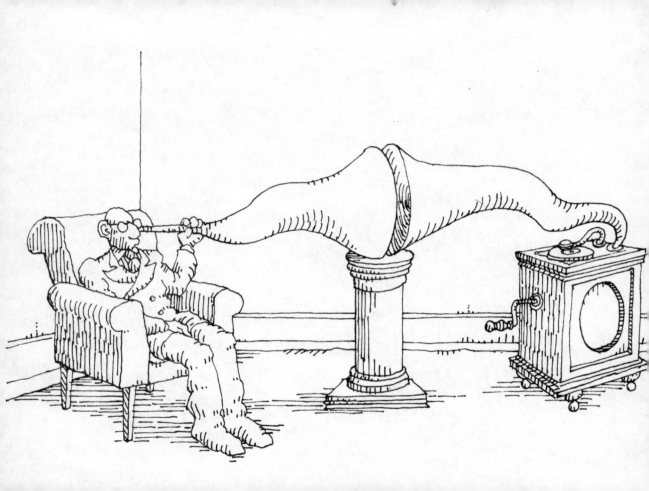

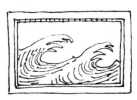

SEA
SICKNESS
BAGS

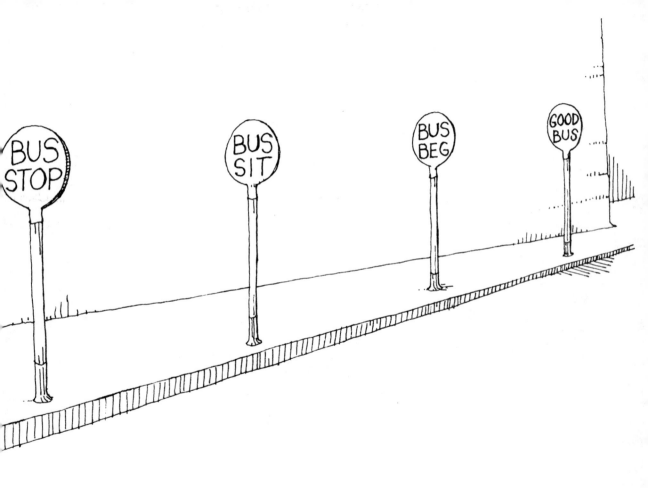

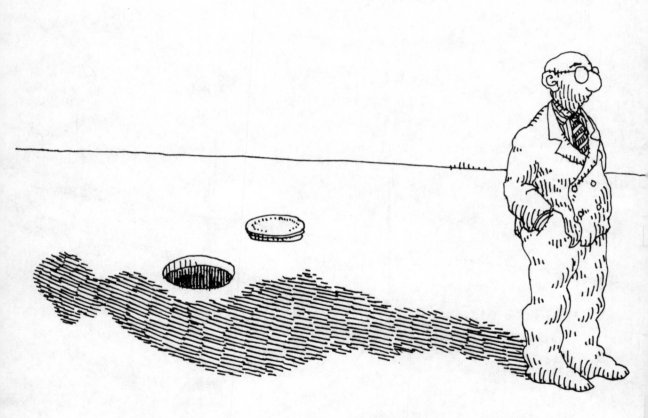

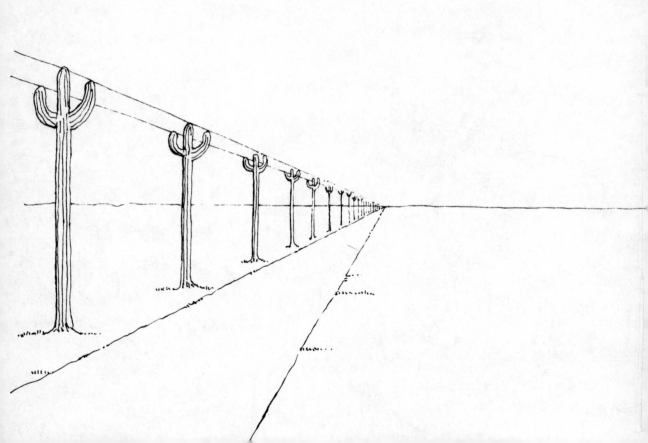

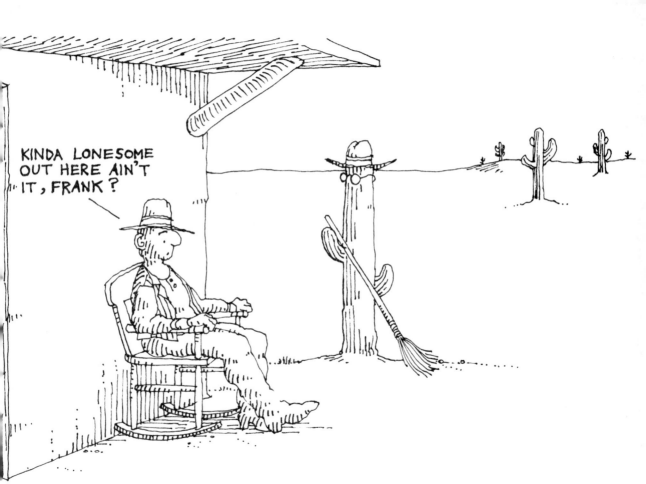

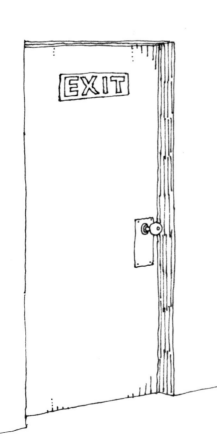

EXIT

ENTER

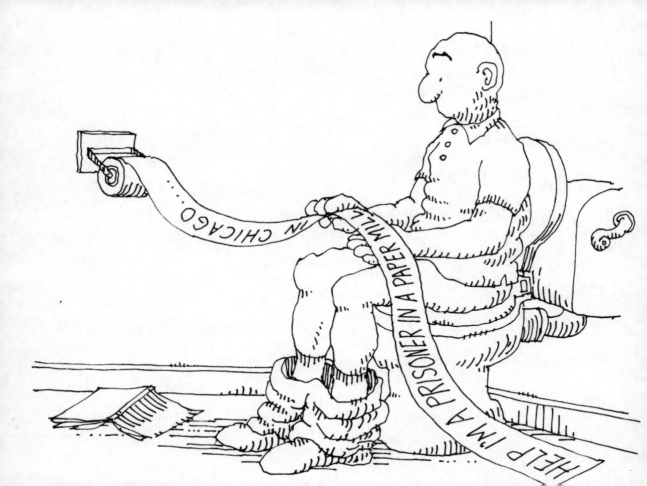

Conceptual Advertising

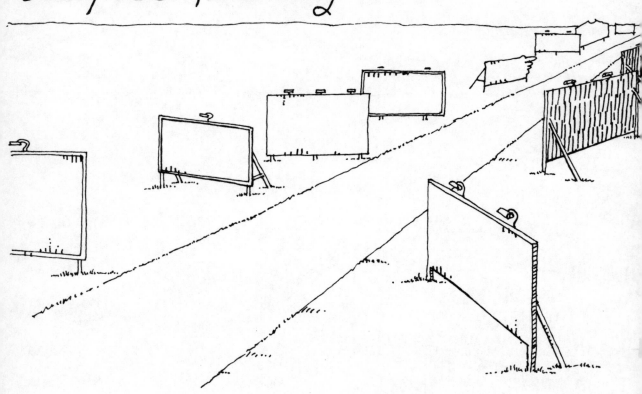

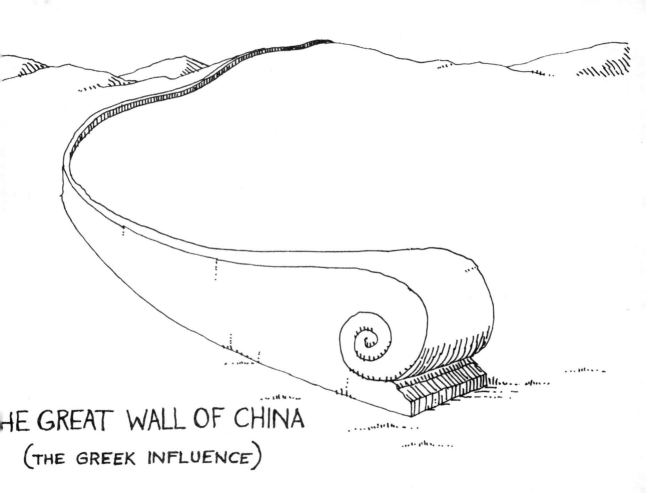

HE GREAT WALL OF CHINA

(THE GREEK INFLUENCE)

PASSOVER ISLAND

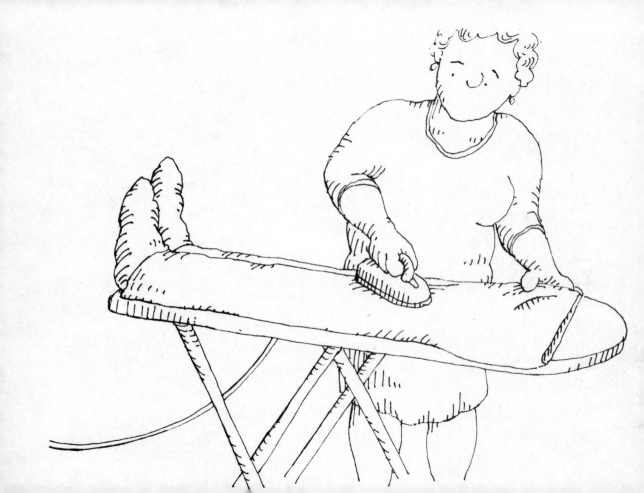

CONCISE
OXFORD
DICTIONARY

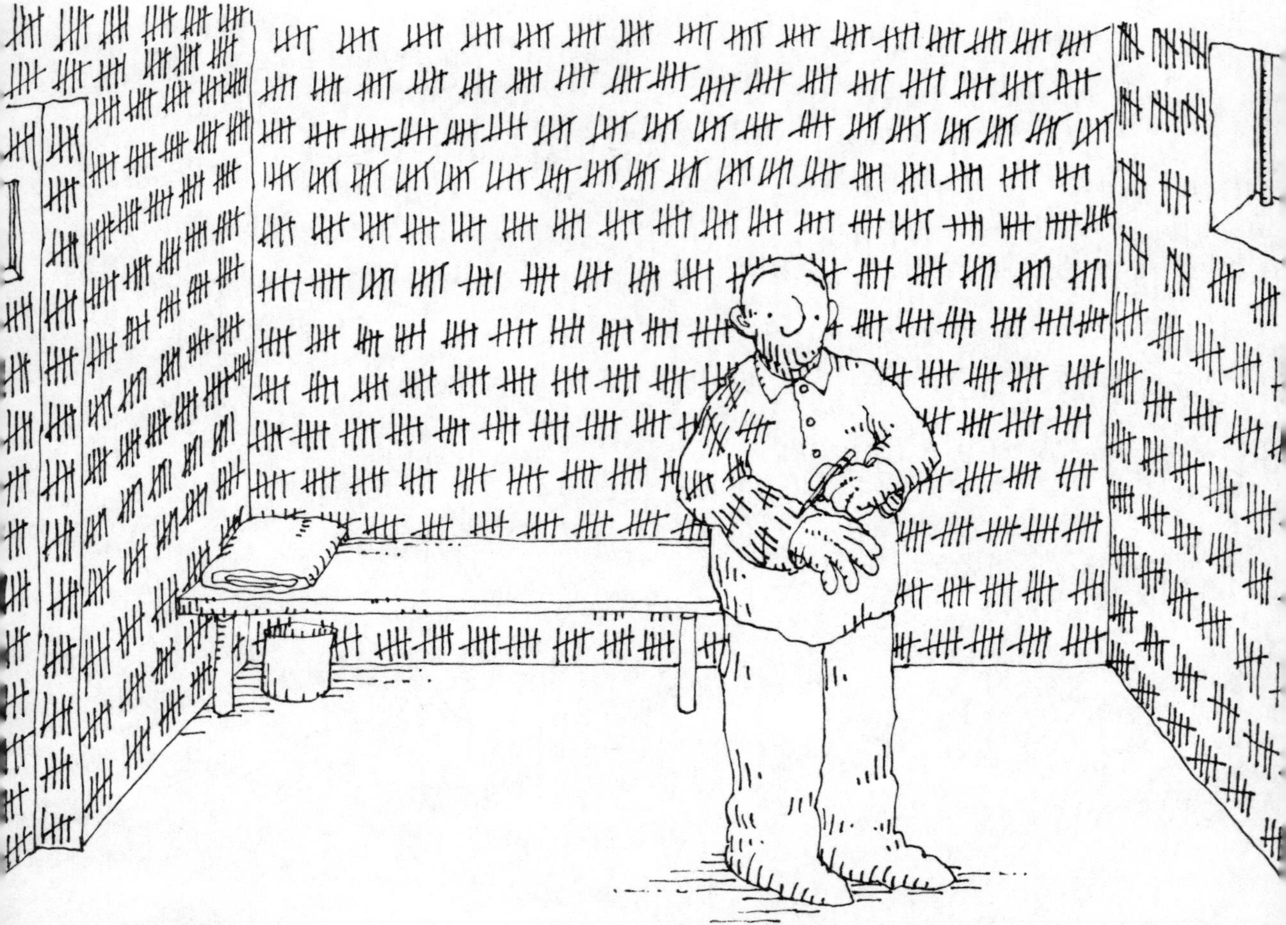

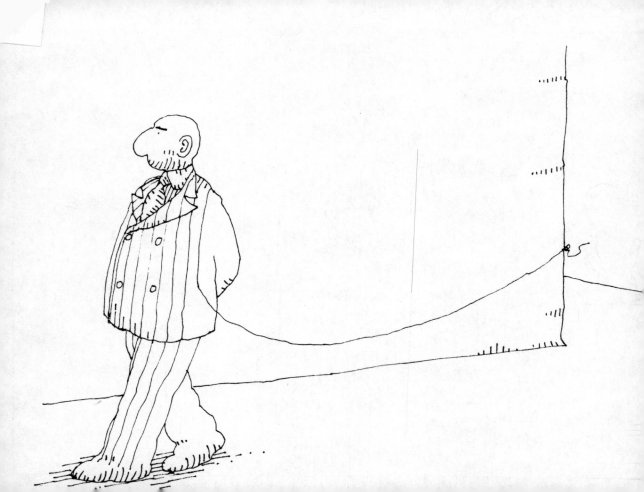

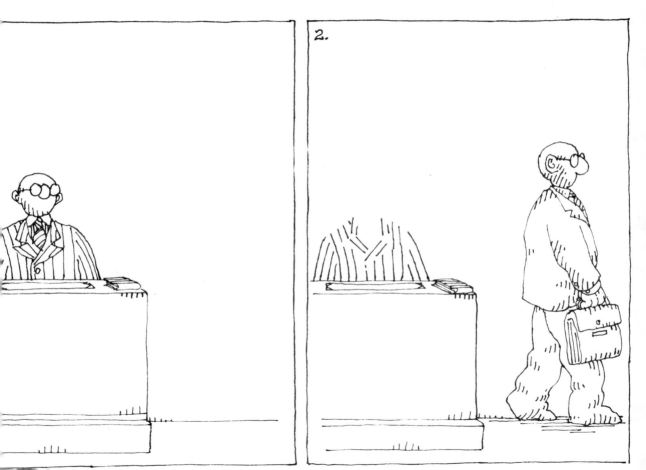

2.

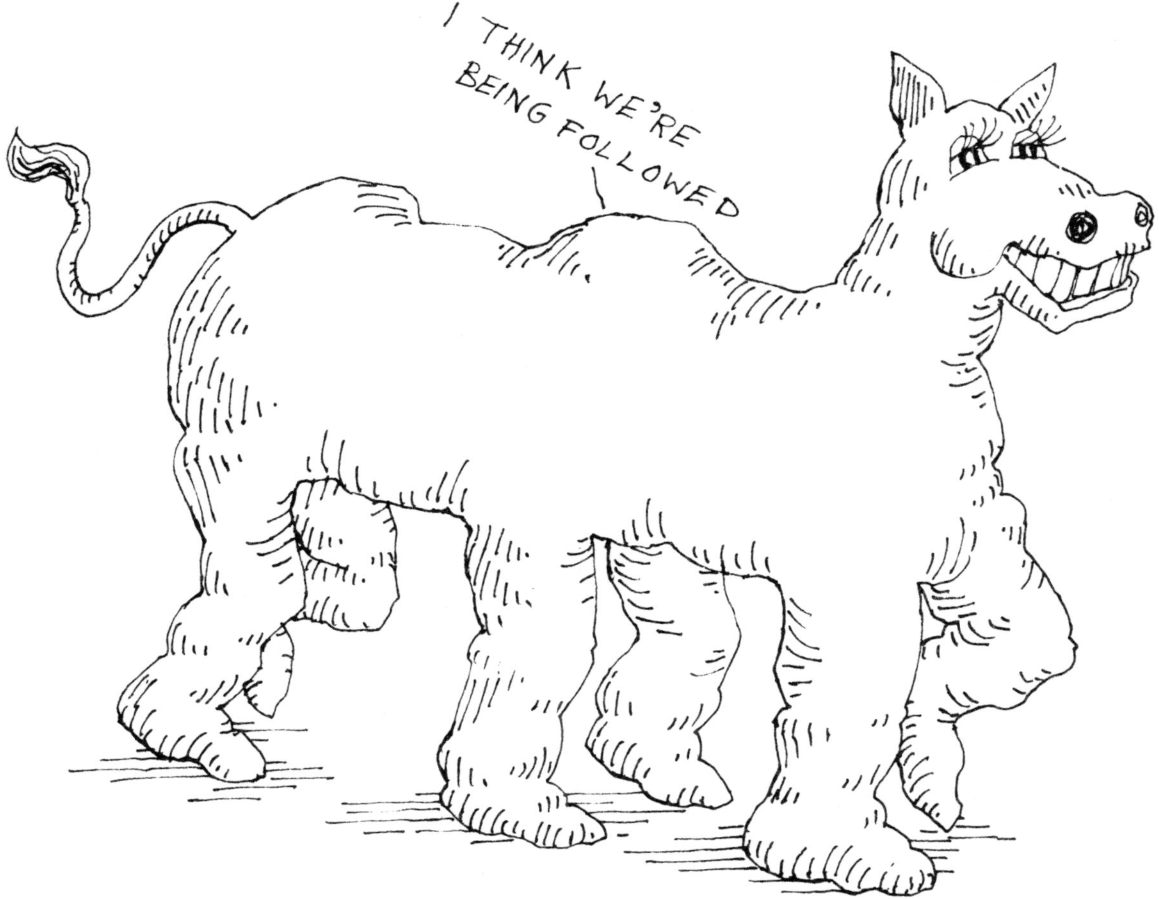
I THINK WE'RE BEING FOLLOWED

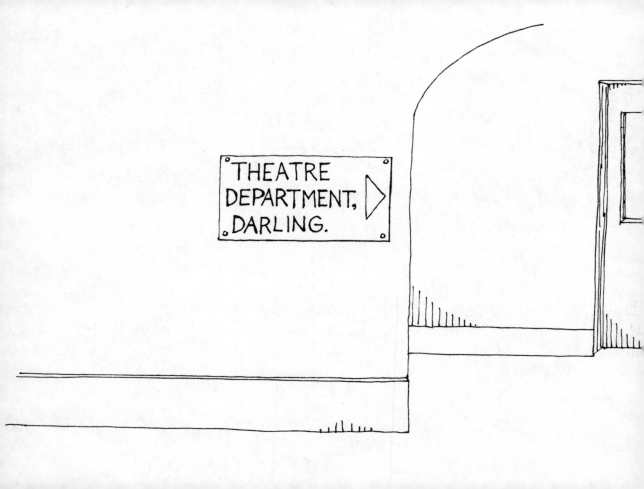

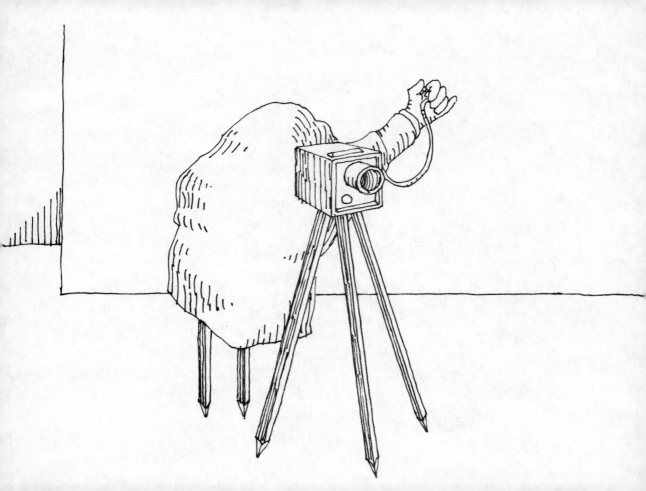

Abraham Lincoln
spoils the
Gettysburg
Address

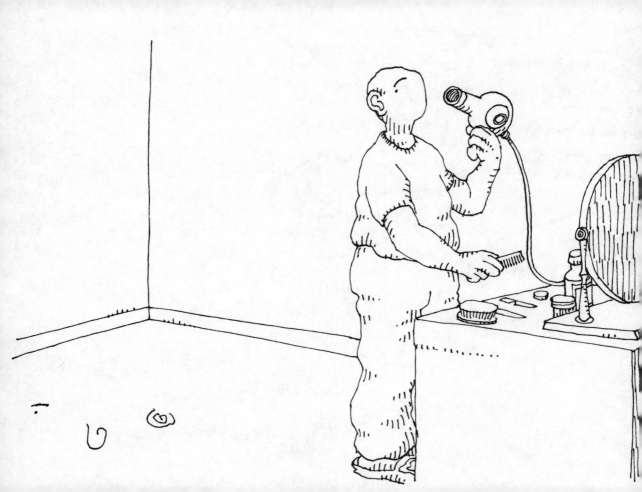

...and you know what
he's like when she doesn't
get her own way... well, I
said to Douglas... Douglas, I said,
tell her we're busy and can't
come over till later... well he
didn't like it... he's not good at
telling tales... especially to her...

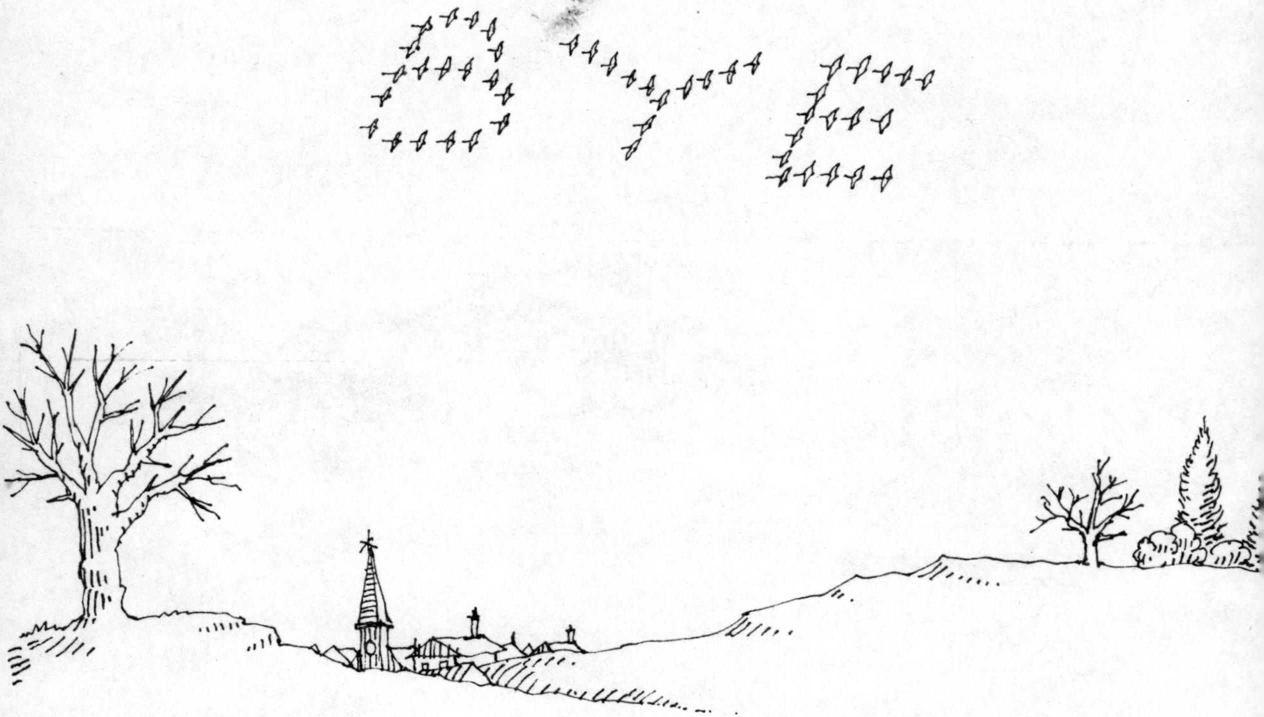